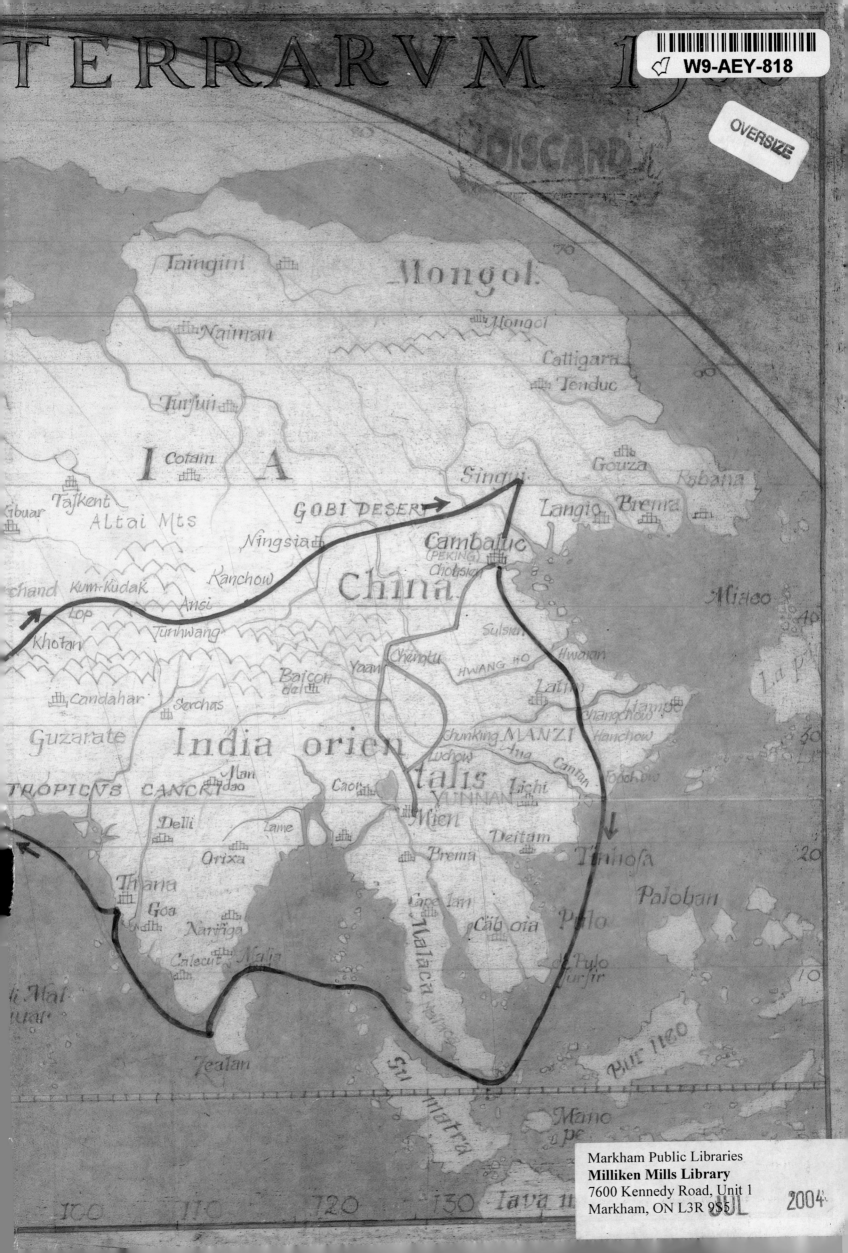

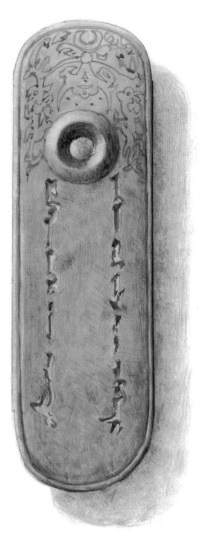

In the 13th century and before, people knew very little about the world outside their own countries. The things that they did know they had only heard from the occasional travelers that passed through. Although Europe and Asia had always been neighbors, their people were not aware of how others looked, what clothes they wore, what language they spoke, or what their land was like. Europeans had seen the beautiful ceramics, jewels, and silk that made their way to them from the Far East, and they had heard about the fabled Silk Road, but no one had actually attempted to go there. It would require someone with a great deal of courage to cross the high mountains and treacherous seas that separated them.

In 1260 the Venetian merchants Matteo Polo and his brother Niccolo sailed out of Venice on a trading trip to the Near East. Their first destination was Constantinople. Sometime during their trip, however, war broke out in the region, disrupting all transport, so they were forced to change their plans. They turned eastward, and after much traveling, eventually arrived in northern China. At the time, the Mongol Emperor, Kublai Khan, whose empire stretched from the Pacific Ocean to the Middle East, ruled China. This empire was considered to be enormous beyond belief.

When the Great Khan set eyes on the two foreigners, with their brown eyes, white skin, and hairy, bearded faces, he was filled with surprised curiosity. He questioned them endlessly about Europe and, on hearing that the people there were mainly Christians, gave the brothers a message for the Pope, which asked for 100 Christian priests to be sent to China. To assist the brothers' safe return, he gave them a gold plate. Presenting this plate at any Mongol command post, they would be able to get food, lodging, and horses.

The return journey was long and difficult. It took three years. They had been away for ten years, and Niccolo's son, Marco, who had been six when they left, was now a young man of 16.

The Pope had died and the brothers had to wait for a new one to be elected before they could pass on the Khan's message. They waited almost two years. When there was time, they talked about their journey and the strange and wonderful things they had seen in China. Marco loved to hold the gleaming gold plate and dream about the far-off land.

The Polo brothers decided not to wait for the election of the new Pope, and in 1271 they set off again for China, by way of Acre. As Marco was fit, strong, and fascinated by China, they took him with them. His life of adventure was about to begin.

English text copyright © 2003
Mason Crest Publishers, Inc.
370 Reed Road
Broomall, Pennsylvania 19008
866-MCP-BOOK (toll-free)
All rights reserved.

Illustrations copyright © 1998 Robert Ingpen
Published in association with
Grimm Press Ltd., Taiwan

1 3 5 7 9 8 6 4 2

Library of Congress Cataloging-in-
Publication Data:

on file at the Library of Congress.

ISBN 1-59084-136-0
ISBN 1-59084-133-6 (series)

Great Names

MARCO POLO

Standing on the dock and peering through the early morning fog, I can almost see on the very far-off horizon that long-imagined, mysterious kingdom my father and uncle have talked so much about. There everything is gold and everyone wears silk; that land is called China.

Since their return, my father and uncle have talked constantly about China, about what strange food the people eat, how strange their language sounds, how they met the Great Khan, and what gifts he gave them. . . . Oh, how I long to see it all for myself.

The first time they left I was only 6. When they returned, I was 16. Now I am 18, and I'm going with them. Oh, happy day! The sails are up! We're about to set sail! Goodbye, Venice!

There are 12 galleys in the fleet, each powered by sails and a crew of oarsmen. Our galley is among them, flying a silver-tasseled pennant, embroidered with three black birds.

We sailed for several days across the Mediterranean and have now arrived in the city of Acre, the western gate of Asia. Soon we will go ashore to buy food, water, horses, and tents for the journey overland. We must travel for two or three years, across lonely mountains and barren deserts, so we must prepare well. Father and Uncle have warned me of the hardships and the dangers, but I am not afraid. I know we will get there—to beautiful, mysterious China.

Father and Uncle promised the Great Khan, whose mother is a Christian, to ask the Pope to send 100 scholars to China to spread the faith. Unfortunately the new Pope, the ex-Bishop of Acre, is unable to send 100 scholars, but he has sent two priests with us and we have some holy oil for the Khan.

As soon as our preparations are complete we will start.

My curiosity knows no bounds. What will we see? What will we encounter on the way?

After several days of traveling, we found ourselves

in the midst of a Sarasen attack, and it seemed we might get trapped in the battle. The priests who were accompanying us were very afraid; instead of trusting God to protect us, they fled back to Acre. Father and Uncle Matteo discussed the situation all night and decided to join a caravan for the rest of the trip east.

The caravan consisted of several hundred horses, camels, and donkeys, as well as guards, guides, and porters. With our party added to it, it looks like a small army, and we feel much safer.

Passing through city after city, we have seen many fascinating things. In one there was a peculiar kind of spring that spat out a black, oily liquid. You can't drink the liquid, but it can be used for fuel. People also smear it onto the skin for rashes and the ulcers of animals. They say it cures disease. Along the way we have used sign language to ask directions. The people are kind and answer us the same way, although gradually we are learning a few words of their languages. The days pass happily. I have begun to record everything I see and hear, so that perhaps this way others will be able to share it with me one day.

Several more weeks of traveling have brought us near the Turkish border. Here steep, narrow mountain paths wind their way between towering cliffs and deep gorges. One small slip and you would never be seen again. Freezing winds whip at us, searing our faces and making progress extremely difficult.

It is said that Noah's Ark landed here, on the top of nearby Mt. Ararat. Since the mountain is covered with snow year-round, and is so tall that none have ever climbed it, the Ark will rest there forever.

Once on the other side of the mountains we found ourselves in an earthly paradise—Persia. Here, there are mosques of the most exquisite design and glorious colors, and gardens in which all kinds of magnificent flowers bloom. The markets are bigger than any markets we have seen; they are full of Persian carpets, fine knives, incense, Chinese porcelain, and silk. It seems the whole world trades here. We spent some time buying goods before moving on.

We have been journeying through increasingly remote areas. No one lives here, and at night the only sound is the howling of the wolves. In the desert, we were caught in a sudden sandstorm. Flying sand and grit turned day to night, and in the darkness the camels' bells clanged in panic. Then we heard the sound of distant horses neighing. "Bandits!" cried my uncle. "Quick, group together."

The horses' hooves pounded in our ears. We drew our swords and began to battle the bandits. The clash of sword on sword, the screams of the wounded and the frightened cries of the animals continued throughout the night, until finally at daybreak it was over. Many were dead and many were wounded, but luckily our family escaped injury. We suffered no more than the loss of some of our goods.

Not long after this, we met up with another caravan and joined them for the rest of the trip. However, I became seriously ill with a fever. The doctor said I would die if I remained in the scorching desert heat. We set off, then, on our own to cross the roof of the world, the Pamir Plateau.

The higher we climbed the colder it got, and my fever began to recede. The path twisted like a snake and was frequently blocked by fallen ice. The air was thin and breathing was difficult. My head ached. What was worse, we couldn't light a fire in this air and we had no way of cooking. We longed for something hot to eat. This was an agony much worse than fever.

It was a long, hard journey to the top, but after finding clean, clear water there, and gradually getting used to the weather, we began to feel much better. Longhaired oxen and long-horned sheep wandered the plateau. The herders used their horns for utensils and even for fences.

Descending from the Pamir Plateau we arrived in Kashgar [today's Xinjinang Province, China], the southern gate to the Silk Road. It is nearly two years since we left Venice and I will soon be 20. The journey has toughened me and given me greater courage.

Leaving Kashgar we passed through a green land of vineyards and cotton fields. The women wore charming hats, and the carpets were bright and colorful. But all this soon gave way to desert again, and when we reached Lop we rested for several days. There, we ate and drank our fill and fed the animals well before gathering supplies for the next leg of the trip. The Gobi Desert lay ahead, and even at its narrowest part it takes 30 days to cross.

Setting off, we had no idea just how harsh the desert would be. With every step it got harder and harder. The sun beat down on us and the wind filled our mouths and noses with sand. Hardly able to open our eyes and parched with thirst, we slumped half-conscious on our camels as they plodded slowly onward. At night we shivered with cold and grew uneasy in the eerie emptiness of the moonlit desert.

They say that people alone in the desert at night often hear something or someone calling their name. This makes them lose all sense of direction. Eventually, confused and lost, they collapse and die in the desert sands. Sometimes we saw the bleached bones of animals half buried in the sand, and we couldn't help but wonder how many lives the desert had consumed. We proceeded with much caution, taking great care of each other so as to avoid any misfortunes.

Thankfully, all went well. After a month, we walked out of the Gobi and with shouts of joy hurried toward the temple's roofs we could make out in the distance. We had arrived in the realm of the Khan [present-day Dunhuang].

There are temples everywhere here, full of statues of many different gods, in wood, clay, and stone, of all sizes. I've seen nothing like them before. There is also a command post, and when they heard we had come to visit the Khan, a message was immediately sent to the next city. Thus, we have received an excellent reception in every city we have passed through. Today were met by a party of officials, sent by the Khan when he heard the news, to escort us to Xanadu.

High marble walls encircle Xanadu
like a giant, white dragon. Inside, amazing
halls stand alongside Mongol tents, amid fragrant
gardens and gently swaying trees. Birds, deer, and
sheep roam the gardens, musicians play on the
Khan's stone boat, and actors perform in the great
square. It is truly an unforgettable sight.

The ministers left us to wash and change. Father
took out a fine suit of velvet clothes brought from
Venice especially for the occasion for me to wear.
But to all our surprise, and through no fault
of mine, it was miles too small.
Three years too small!

On entering the palace, the first thing I saw were the ranks of black-clad royalty, aristocracy, officials, warriors, and palace attendants, all of whom were staring at us with wide-eyed wonder. Advancing further, I could see the Khan on his gold throne. A lion lay at his feet, affirming his authority and power. In common with the Mongols I had already seen, he had tan skin, black hair, and dark eyes, but such eyes, piercing and all-knowing like an eagle's!

In accordance with Chinese etiquette, we knelt before him and touched our heads three times to the ground before presenting the holy oil and other gifts we had brought. Father and Uncle Matteo then gave him an account of our journey, to which he listened very attentively. From time to time his eyes flicked over me, assessing me. I returned his look without fear. After three years of imagining what he was like, I was finally seeing him. Outwardly he looked rather fierce, but his manner was warm and I liked him.

When he heard about my fever and how I had nearly died, he smiled and called me a courageous young man. Then he turned to my father.

"Your son, Marco, is clever. I would like to keep him here as my attendant. Do you agree?"

I agreed immediately, certain that I would learn a great deal in his service, and Father gave his permission. Very pleased, the Khan presented us with many precious gifts. These meant little to me, however, for I was too excited by the new life I was about to begin.

I went with the Great Khan back to Beijing. Beijing was even grander, lovelier, and more prosperous than Xanadu. I was fascinated by the goods for sale in the markets, where they were made, and their prices. I discovered the Chinese used paper money for trading, something I'd never seen in Europe. The Great Khan regularly sent me to different parts of his realm to investigate and report on conditions there. He loved to hear me describe what the local people ate, what they wore, and what unusual plants or animals there were in the region.

In Hangzhou, Chin's largest port, life is very good. A city of 12,000 bridges and more than a million inhabitants, it hosts doctors, fortunetellers, artisans, and every kind of profession. Trade has brought them prosperity and a life of luxury. Almost everyone wears silk and adorns themselves with pearls.

From a wharf on the Yangtze River, I tried to count the hundreds of boats that pass each hour. The goods they carry are worth more than the entire wealth of Venice. The local governments along the river grow rich from the taxes on them.

Leaving Hagzhou, we headed, via Chang'an, for Sichuan, Yunnan, and Tibet and the regions bordering Burma, Vietnam, and India. The life of the people we meet seems similar to that of the Chinese, except that their food is very spicy. I saw people with gold-coated teeth, and snakes that could swallow a man in one bite. I also saw a tree that if you cut through its bark, bleeds a fluid that dries to form frankincense. There are so many new and amazing things to remember, and I record them all carefully so I can tell the Great Khan about them on my return to Beijing.

It is many years now since I first came to China and I am so used to the Chinese way of life, I am almost becoming Chinese.

Not long after my return from a recent trip, a revolt broke out among the Mongols in Manchuria. The Great Khan personally led his army into battle. It was the first time I had ever been on a battlefield and seen for myself the slaughter and bloodshed that takes place there. Are all these splendid palaces and prosperous cities built on a river of blood?

Sitting on the riverbank, watching the sunset and its gold-red reflection in the water, I suddenly feel a strong longing for home—Venice's canals, its gondolas, its wine. We've been in China for 17 years; I'm middle-aged, and Father and Uncle Matteo are growing old.

Tonight we talked a lot about home and decided it was time to return. Moreover, an opportunity has presented itself. The King of Persia has sent his messengers to the Khan to discuss a marriage between their families, and the Khan has agreed. He has promised the princess to him as his bride, but because of fighting in Central Asia, he is worried about her safety on the way to Persia. Summoning my courage, I have offered to escort her by sea.

Knowing we were born and bred in a port, the Great Khan accepted readily. He is having 13 large junks specially made and has ordered more than 3,000 soldiers to accompany us.

De leſtoille de mer.

Eſte eſtoille de mer qui ne ſe
uoit une autie au contaire
les mauuaiſe ꝑ cela ꝑ cel
quelle naꝑeit point anꝑꝯ·
ꝑt a eulr murꝑuꝯ on

Father and Uncle Matteo are overwhelmed with happiness. They have packed their belongings and exchanged all their goods for gold, silver, pearls, and jewels. Sea travel is unsafe, and as nearly 20 years of hardship and endeavor are tied up in these valuables, we have taken the precaution of sewing them into our clothes.

In 1293 our fleet sailed out of Quanzhou harbor. As the land receded, our sorrow at leaving grew.

The long sea voyage was full of danger. Sometimes we were buffeted by huge storm waves, and everyone was so ill that even drowning seemed a better fate. Sometimes we had to land on isolated islands to wait for the arrival of the trade winds. Those who were not used to the heat suffered badly.

We sailed for two whole years before we finally reached the Persian port of Hormuz. Once there, we discovered that the King had died, and even more astonishing, that the Great Khan too had passed away. I felt sadly bereaved.

In accordance with Mongol customs, we delivered the princess to the King's son. Then, our mission complete, we set off overland to the Black Sea. Afterward, we went by boat back to Venice, where we landed in 1295.

At the first sight of home, our eyes filled with tears. We had been gone 24 years! Our memories of Venice flooded back.

We took a gondola home. The gondolier couldn't take his eyes off us; we realized that no one would believe that we were Venetians returning home. Our skin was black from the sun, full beards hid our faces, and our clothes were outlandish. We couldn't even speak the language fluently. Our own servants thought we were thieves and tried to turn us away from the house. It took a lot of convincing before we were happily reunited with our family. Clearly, it is going to take some time before everyone accepts us again.

Three days after our arrival, we held a big banquet at the house, and in front of all the guests, we cut open our tattered clothes to reveal the glittering jewels and gold beneath. Breaking the stunned silence that followed, we began to explain who we were and what had happened to us. Realizing that we were indeed the three lost Polos, there were cries of of amazement at our riches. That is how I got the nickname Millionaire Marco.

I settled down, married, and had a family. I worked hard at my business and was successful. But after a mere two years of the peaceful, happy life, war broke out between Venice and neighboring Ravenna for control of sea trade. I could not stand by and see my homeland humiliated, so I lead my family's ships into the war. Our merchant ships had no experience in war, and although we fought well, we were defeated. I was captured and taken to Ravenna, where I was imprisoned. In the gloomy jail, my past adventures came back to me with even greater clarity, and I frequently told them to an eager audience of fellow prisoners.

A fellow prisoner, a writer named Rustichello, wrote a book of my experiences. Although there were some who found it hard to believe, I actually didn't include the most fantastic things that I saw!

My hope is that my experiences will bridge the deep divide between Europe and Asia, that later generations of explorers will follow in my footsteps and continue to explore this new world, for the further we travel, the bigger our world becomes.

BIOGRAPHIES

Author John Riddle is a freelance author from Bear, Delaware. His byline has appeared in the *Washington Post,* the *New York Times, Boston Magazine,* and dozens of other publications. He is the author of *Consulting Business* and *Streetwise Guide to Business Management.* He is a frequent speaker at writing conferences around the country.

Illustrator Robert Ingpen is a master illustrator who was the first Australian to win the International Hans Christian Anderson Award. He creates children's stories with beautiful illustrations. He put to use his knowledge of the humanities and natural sciences in painting the illustrations, and he blended into his works his love for children, affection for the land, and respect for all living creatures. Interestingly, Ingpen's illustrations sometimes have inspired scientists to explore and study the subject from new perspectives. This is where the charm of Ingpen lies.

TYPVS ORBIS